DIY
style

*Create your own cool &
original stuff*

KAREN COOPER

SCHOLASTIC INC.

New York   Toronto   London   Auckland   Sydney
Mexico City   New Delhi   Hong Kong   Buenos Aires

Thanks to Mum and Gram for passing along the DIY gene!

No part of this publication may be reproduced in whole or in part, or stored in a retrieval system, or transmitted in any form or by any means, electronic, mechanical, photocopying, recording, or otherwise, without written permission of the publisher. For information regarding permission, write to The Chicken House, 2 Palmer Street, Frome, Somerset BA11 1DS, United Kingdom.

ISBN 0-439-33888-3

Text © 2002 by Karen Cooper.
Illustrations © 2002 by Nicola Cramp.

All rights reserved. Published by Scholastic Inc., 557 Broadway, New York, NY 10012. The Chicken House is published in the United States in association with Scholastic.

SCHOLASTIC and associated logos are trademarks and/or registered trademarks of Scholastic Inc. THE CHICKEN HOUSE and associated logos are trademarks of The Chicken House.

12 11 10 9 8 7 6 5 4 3 2 1   2 3 4 5 6 7/0

Printed in the U.S.A.
First Scholastic printing, May 2002

CONTENTS

INTRODUCTION	7
DIY style!	8
What is style?	10
Style quiz	12

Part 1: FASHION FORWARD	20

1 Awesome Accessories — 22

Beaded coil bracelet	23
Beaded belt	25
Hipster chain-link belt	27
Knotted choker	28
Chic sequin choker	31
Glitter-gal hair clip	33
Blooming ponytail holder	34
Handbag hoopla	36
Head scarf	39
Cool cuff bracelet	40

2 Retro-a-go-go — 42

Flip-flop fun	43
"Vintage" cropped jeans	45
Denim & ribbon redo	47
Studded duds	48

Sassy sleeveless T-neck   50
Beaded T   52
5 fab ways to wear a feather boa!   53
More fun and funky DIY style tricks!   55

3 Divine Decorating 58

A little something about
color   59
Pillow magic   61
Beaded curtain   63
Bead-dazzling lamp shade 65
Fab "fur" phone   66
Decorative drawer knobs   67
Cool canopy bed   69
Flower-power light string   71
Custom corkboard   72
More fun uses for a feather boa   74
Ancient Feng Shui secrets!   75

Part 2: LIFE-"STYLE"   78

4 Lotions & Potions 80

Essential info on essential
oils   81
"Peppy"-mint cleansing
bar   85
Chunky soap cubes   87

Refreshing citrus scent 89

Luscious lip balm 90

All that glitters gel 93

Bath bomb 94

Vanilla swirl bubble bath 95

Soothing eye pillow 96

Smoothing body scrub 98

5 *Gifty Goodies* **100**

Lavender mini pillows 101

Totally custom journal 103

"Fab"-ric vase 105

Origami gift box 108

Gifty baskets 110

Cookie cutter gift cards 113

More cool card ideas 115

Wrap it up! 116

6 *Entertaining* **118**

Introduction 119

Hawaiian luau party 128

Chocolate decadence party 137

Afternoon tea party 142

Far-out, Far East festivity 151

It's a wrap! 159

INTRODUCTION

Before beginning any of the projects in this book, **MAKE SURE YOU GET THE OK FROM YOUR PARENTS!** It can be a drag to find out that you've cut up your mom's favorite dress after you've already turned it into a groovy purse. And it's ALWAYS a good idea when using things like scissors, adhesives, sewing needles, and especially the stove or oven to have someone older around to make sure there are no fingers accidentally glued together or burned, etc. Now, with the friendly caution aside — fasten your seat belt and get ready for an all-out DIY style blitz!

DIY
style!

E ver find yourself flipping through your favorite fashion mags or shopping in your best-loved stores and totally craving all those cute, quirky, totally style-forward things that just scream "you"? Well, the good news is that you don't have to be in the latest all-girl band or the daughter of an A-list movie star in order to get your hands on the latest and greatest in today's style. With a little imagination, a smidgen of time, and lots of stuff you can find around the house, you can get the look yourself with ***DIY style!*** Inside you'll find inspiration for everything from trendy

accessories and clothing updates to bedroom redos, super-easy soaps and lotions, party ideas, and tons more! Plus, to help you out on selecting the perfect project, you'll find materials lists, difficulty ratings, DIY tips, and reviews from girls themselves. Best of all, every tried-and-true **DIY style** project gives you ideas on how to add your own one-of-a-kind spin for a totally personalized look that's all **YOU**! So even if you haven't picked up a pair of scissors since fifth grade art class, you're sure to find projects that you and your friends make, keep, share, and more. With **DIY style**, you'll make "homemade" hip! (But heck, if you want everyone to think you picked up your groovy goodies at that trendy boutique in town, we're not going to tell!)

WHAT IS *style?*

S tyle — you know what it is when you see it, but what exactly is style? When most of us think of style, we tend to think of the latest fashion trends — what's hip, what's hot at the moment — but style is way more than just a look. Style is a way of being — **your** way of being — that comes through in everything you do, say, wear — whatever! A favorite necklace,

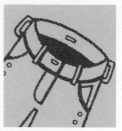

a perfectly worn pair of jeans, your perfume, how you wear your hair, your favorite expressions, the things that decorate your room — style is that something that makes a statement about who you are before you even say one word.

The big thing to remember is there's no limit to or restrictions on what your personal style can be. Maybe you're a forever glam princess or as style-moody as Madonna (Material Girl, Earth Mother, Cowgirl — you name it, she's been it!),

classic

retro

glam

hippie

what's important is that your style is fun, fresh, and says something about the one-of-a-kind gal you are!

Style is:

★ Fun
★ Easy
★ Affordable
★ Confidence-giving
★ Expressive
★ Inspired
★ YOU!

Style is NOT:

✪ Ultraserious
✪ Expensive
✪ Difficult
✪ Limited
✪ About being a "copycat"!

This last one is a biggie — while it's great to be inspired by someone's sense of style (think of the belly-baring style revolutionized by Britney Spears!),

totally copying her look can be, well, totally tacky. Back in the '80s when Madonna first broke on to the scene, swarms of girls around the world started sporting her funky lace gloves, poufy short skirt, messy highlighted hair, rubber bracelets, and off-the-shoulder *Flashdance* shirt — and they wore them all at once. They even penciled in their own above-the-lip beauty mark — yikes! Needless to say, they looked pretty ridiculous. Sure, going with one of those looks and blending it in with your own fashion mix can make a hip statement, but imitating the entire look pretty much says "Happy Halloween." Stay true to your style first!

*Style*QUIZ

*N*ot sure about your style? Are you a quintessential Classic Miss, total Hippie Chick, funky Retro Girl, the ultimate Glam Diva, or super Sports Goddess? Take our *DIY Style* quiz to uncover your current style status!

1 **Congratulations! You've just won two tickets to anywhere in the world! Which** of the following locales is most likely to show up on your dream destination list?

   a) Chez Paris
   b) Exotic India
   c) I Love New York
   d) Action-packed LA
   e) Rocky Mountain High
   f) None of the above.

2 **When you were younger, you were most likely to do which of the** following with a coloring book:

   a) Color perfectly inside the lines using complementary hues.
   b) Coloring book? You'd rather draw your own pictures, thank you!
   c) Save it as a memento of your youth.
   d) Wish you had that new "Beauty Secrets Barbie" to play with instead.
   e) Use it as a baseball bat.
   f) None of the above.

3 You've just got your big break to sing backup with your favorite female artist — who would you be most likely to tour with?

    a) Jessica Simpson

    b) Jewel

    c) Nelly Furtado

    d) Christina Aguilera

    e) Sing backup? You'd rather back up Mia Hamm on the soccer field!

    f) None of the above.

4 Your dream home would have you setting up camp where?

    a) A cute little cottage by the coast.

    b) A hut in Tahiti.

    c) A renovated warehouse loft.

    d) A luxury uptown penthouse.

    e) A cozy cabin in the woods.

    f) None of the above.

5 Your idea of the ultimate first date with your new crush would be:

    a) An afternoon sailing in your beau's new boat.

    b) An outdoor acoustic music festival.

c) An all-day trip to a giant flea market.

d) An all-day trip to a massive mall.

e) A super slam-dunk contest.

f) None of the above.

6 **You're most likely to dedicate your free time to which of the following causes:**

a) Saving for a French manicure.

b) Saving the rain forest.

c) Saving old LPs.

d) Saving Britney and Justin's relationship.

e) Saving your energy for a 5K road race.

f) None of the above.

MOSTLY

Classic miss

 Badminton, anyone? Your refined style is all about clean, simple lines and classic colors. Black and white are total musts for your wardrobe — and navy only if you're feeling daring. This uncomplicated, no-fuss style carries over into everything from your hair (a one-length bob, perhaps?) to your simple bedroom decorations. You'd rather

spend an afternoon in the dentist's chair than be caught dead wearing fluorescent nail polish.

MOSTLY B

Hippie chick

Peace, love, and patchouli! Your earthy style is free and flowing, patterned by exotic colors, textures, and of course, natural fabrics. Hemp is your hands-down accessory of choice. Hippie chicks like you prefer to avoid the status quo and decorate with unusual pieces from all over the world. Your style standby? A tossed-on T-shirt, long flowered skirt, and head scarf. Style opposite? Anything that even resembles a suit.

MOSTLY C

Retro girl

Happy days! Your quirky retro style borrows the best from yesteryear and mixes it with what's hot today. Your favorite hangout? Vintage stores where you can find the perfect pieces to create your groovy and

diverse look. Never scared to experiment, you can incorporate almost anything into your style and make it work. Your biggest fear? Being caught out on the town without your funky trademark accessories!

MOSTLY D

Glam diva

The spotlight's on you! Anything that's shiny, glitzy, attention-getting — that's what you're about. If they're wearing it in tinseltown, you're wearing it at home. Up on the latest styles, you read fashion mags like they're instruction manuals. The key is finding a glam look that's right for you. Worst night-mare? Blending into the crowd.

MOSTLY E

Sports goddess

You're all about high-five style! Your look? Stuff that's cool and comfortable, with a definite athletic edge. Whether you're picking up the latest pair of running shoes or

throwing your hair into a quick 'n' easy ponytail, style for you has to be about function. You
score best with a less-is-more attitude and
have no time for major high-maintenance
anything.

Style maverick

 Yee-haw! You're off exploring
the wild frontiers and breaking
new ground when it comes to
personal style. Independent in
nature, no one's going to classify you, no siree.
Instead, style is an open road waiting for you
to ride it with whatever completely individual
look you choose!

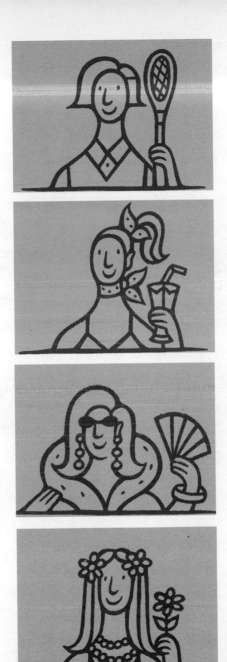

PART I

FASHION FORWARD

*W*hether you're into jazzing up your personal look or updating the look of your room, we've got some fun projects to make your style sizzle! In this section, you'll find the complete how-tos for the fun style-dos — no matter what your style status. From cool bracelets and head scarves to bead-dazzling bedroom makeover tips and beyond — you can get the look you're after even on the smallest style budget. Best yet, most of these projects can be done in less than an hour — but don't rush! Patience is key when it comes to any DIY project — and it'll show in the quality of the finished product. Plus, the fun is in the creating. (OK, and in the wearing, decorating . . .) But remember, these are total

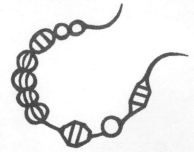

*DIY*style

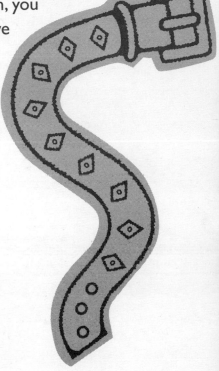

guidelines to get you started — don't be afraid to experiment and put your own spin on things to make it truly yours! Who knows, by the time you finish, you may never have to buy another belt, bracelet, or bedroom decoration again! (And a jar of glue may have become your next best friend!)

Chapter 1

Awesome Accessories

Accessorize, accessorize, accessorize — the mantra of any true style goddess!

$\mathcal{G}$roovy bracelets, cool belts, hot hair clips — it's these kinds of fresh 'n' fun accessories that totally "make" the outfit. Here are some simple projects that will give you the latest looks at a fraction of the cost — plus ideas on how you can customize them to totally fit your own personal style requirements!

Bead magic!

Beads, beads, beautiful beads! There're wood beads, metallic beads, crystal beads, clay beads — more beads than a single girl could ever hope for. So make sure to pick colors, shapes, and textures that appeal to you! Check out bead stores or craft shops for the best variety.

Beaded coil bracelet

Beaded bracelets are hot, but this cool coil shape definitely adds a li'l something extra. And making these trendy bracelets is so fun and easy that you can do them with friends or on your own. Make them, share them, trade them!

Materials list
- ✔ Seed beads
- ✔ Fine-gauge wire
  (that comes in a coil)
- ✔ Needle-nose pliers

1 Clip one end of the wire from the coil. (Where you clip the wire will determine how many coils will be in your finished bracelet.)

2 Using the pliers, curl up one end of the wire at the very tip (this will keep the beads from sliding off the wire).

3 Add beads one at a time, starting at the opposite end. Carefully push beads around the coils to the end.

4 Leave a small length at the end and curl up the wire, using the pliers.

Beaded belt

Turn your favorite beads into a simple but funky belt for some super style! And if you get tired of using it as a belt you can always tie it around your neck and turn it into a hip lariat necklace. Talk about style-convertible!

Materials list
- ✔ Seed beads or other small beads
- ✔ 2 larger beads
- ✔ String or embroidery thread

1 Wrap the string around your waist for sizing. Add about 18 inches on to your waist size and cut.

2 Knot one end of the string and add on one of the larger beads.

3 Continue stringing with the smaller beads until you have about 2 inches left of string remaining.

4 Add the second larger bead and knot the string. (You may need to double the knot to make sure the bead doesn't slide off!)

5 Slide through belt loops or wrap around your waist, tie, and let the ends hang for full-on fashion fun!

Difficulty rating ✂

TIP: Try putting the beads on in patterns. Use different color groupings to add some extra style!

Hipster chain-link belt

Style inspiration can come from anywhere — including hardware stores!

Check out this trendy hip-hanging chain belt — you've seen them all over the fashion mags — now you can see one in your closet! Ours is cheap, groovy, and easy to make. And hardware stores generally sell a variety of metals and link sizes on spools — so finding a perfect chain to match your look is a breeze. Best yet, you don't even need a tool belt to make it!

Materials list
- ✔ Length of chain
- ✔ Sturdy jewelry clasp
- ✔ Pliers

1 Your first step starts at the local hardware store! Pick a chain you like, wrap it around your hips to a length that you want your belt to be. Be sure to leave a little extra hanging for a totally trendy look. The hardware store salesperson will be able to cut the chain for you.

2 Use the pliers to attach one side of the clasp to the last link on the chain.

3 Attach the other side of the clasp to the position where you'd like the belt to close — remember to let it hang slightly!

4 That's it! Clasp and wear.

Difficulty rating ✂ ✂

 TIP: This look works great with a T-shirt and slim-fitting jeans.

Knotted choker

All you need is some thread and beads to create this total-style staple. For a more glam look, choose bright-colored or glittery thread, or try some hemp cording and a wooden bead for a more earthy feel. The bead works to create the clasp.

1 Cut two strands of thread or cording to a length that reaches three times around your neck. Fold the strands in half to make four lengths of thread.

2 Tie a knot near the top of the folded strands (your bead will need to fit snugly through to create a fastener — like a button).

3 Bring the right two cords over the left two cords.

4 Bring the right cords behind the left cords and then through the loop formed on the right, making a loose knot.

5 Now, bring the left cords over the right cords.

6 Bring the left cords behind the right cords and then through the loop on the left side.

7 Continue to tie knots from left to right. Finish your choker by slipping a bead over the four strands and tying off with a knot. Slip the bead through the end loops to fasten.

Difficulty rating
✄ ✄ ✄

TIP: More high style from a hardware store! Link together a series of medium-sized metal washers with ribbon for an "industrial" choker. Or loop a piece of ribbon halfway through a single large washer; repeat with another piece and tie behind your neck. Also, poke around fabric shops or even flea markets for charms, beads, clasps, and buttons that make a great focal point for a choker.

Chic sequin choker

Looking for something a little more glammy in your choice of chokers? Add some sparkle to your look with this simple 'n' chic sequin choker. You can find inexpensive sequins at fabric or craft shops, or get Mom's OK to poke through her closet for an old sequin piece that's seen better days. You can choose one shade of sequins for a more monochrome look or liven things up with a few different colors!

Materials list

✔ Sequins
✔ A few medium-sized beads
✔ Elastic thread
✔ Ruler

1 Wrap the elastic thread around your neck so it fits loosely (sure it's called a choker, but you don't want to cut off your circulation — even if it's in the name of style!).

2 Add 2 inches to the length of the elastic and cut. So if your neck measures 12 inches, cut a piece of elastic 14 inches long.

3 Tie a knot at one end so the sequins don't slide off when you start stringing them.

4 Now this is where a little planning comes into play. It's time to decide what you want your choker pattern to be. Maybe you want a ¼ inch of one color sequin, then a bead, and another set of color. Or maybe you want to vary the color of every sequin? Pick a pattern that's fairly simple for your first try.

5 Now it's time to start adding sequins! Begin stringing the sequins on the thread by sliding the thread through the center hole. Some sequins have a slight curve to them, so make sure they're all facing the same direction when you put them on.

6 Continue adding sequins followed by a bead based on your pattern. Definitely don't drive yourself nuts by trying to count sequins to make the pattern even — you can tell just by "eyeballing" it.

7 When you have about 2 inches of thread remaining, wrap the choker (carefully!) around

your neck to see how it fits. If it's tight, add some more sequins until it's comfortable. If it's too loose, you can take off a few sequins.

8 You're almost there! Now it's time to tie the two ends of elastic together in a knot. Make sure you tie as closely to the beginning and end of the sequins as possible for the best fit.

Difficulty rating ✂ ✂

TIP: Try making a matching bracelet by making the elastic 2 inches longer than your wrist and following your pattern!

Glitter-gal hair clip

Adding some subtle style to your look couldn't be easier! You've probably seen these glitter clips going for tons of money in accessory shops — but wait until you find out how easy they are to make!

Materials list
✔ Plain hair clips
✔ Clear nail polish
✔ Glitter
✔ Scissors

1 Apply clear polish to the outside of the hair clip. Make sure to coat it well!

2 Sprinkle glitter so it completely covers the clip.

3 Next, shake off excess glitter (and save it for the next barrette!).

4 Once the polish has dried, apply another coat or two of polish over the top of the clip to protect.

Groovy glitter-gal style in minutes!

Difficulty rating ✂ ✂

Blooming ponytail holder

There's no doubt that faux flowers are the hottest accessory around. Here's a quick and easy way to turn the basic ponytail elastic into full-bloom style. Choose a few smaller flowers for a more refined look or a large brightly colored bloom for a bigger style statement.

Materials list

✔ Ponytail holder
✔ 1 fabric flower
   (including leaves)
✔ Strong fabric glue
✔ Scissors

1 Cut the flower head from the stem as close to the base of the flower head as possible (the flatter the base of the flower head, the better!).

2 Cut one of the leaves off the remaining stem.

3 Slip the ponytail holder over the leaf, so it rests in the middle of the leaf. Take the fabric glue and dab a bit on each end of the leaf. Affix the leaf (with the ponytail holder still in the middle) to the back of the flower head.

4 Let glue set according to the instructions on the tube, and get ready for blooming ponytail beauty!

You can also try attaching flowers to hair clips! Just make

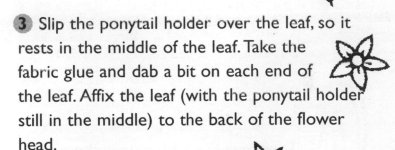

sure the back of the flower is cut flat so you can securely glue it to the outside of a clip.

TIP: Your ponytail holder can double as a bow on packages to friends! Just wrap the elastic around the box for small gift boxes, or tape to the top of larger presents.

Handbag hoopla

ADULT HELP NEEDED!

Now you can make adorable little bags to go with all your looks! Just choose some fun fabric, a little trim, cording for the strap, and get ready to sew 'n' go! And the great thing is you can decorate your bag any way you like. For some flirty fun, stitch a few faux flowers onto your finished bag or add a few beads for a more "sophisticated" look that's oh-so-vogue!

Materials list

- ✔ 16 x 8-inch piece of fabric
- ✔ 10 inches cording
  (available at fabric shops)
- ✔ 1 x 8-inch-length
  ribbon or trim
- ✔ Fabric flowers, beads,
  buttons, etc.
- ✔ Embroidery thread
- ✔ Pins
- ✔ Thread
- ✔ Needle
- ✔ Scissors
- ✔ Ruler

1 Using a ruler, draw two 8 x 8-inch squares on the fabric and cut them out.

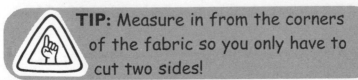

TIP: Measure in from the corners of the fabric so you only have to cut two sides!

2 Next, pin together the two squares, leaving one side open. Make sure the front or decorated sides of the fabric are facing each other when you pin them together.

3 If you aren't a super-sewer, get an adult to help you sew the two pieces together, either by hand or with a sewing machine. Turn inside out.

4 Stitch the ends of the cording to the top of the bag to create the strap.

5 Sew some ribbon or fun trim along the top edge to keep it from unraveling (plus it looks really cool). The basic bag is complete!

6 Try adding more trim, a few beads, buttons, flowers — whatever makes the bag yours!

Difficulty rating ✂ ✂ ✂ ✂

I needed some help from my mom on the sewing part – but I love my new bag! My friends all ask where I got it!

Bonnie, 11

Head scarf

A hip new head scarf is just a few stitches away!

Materials list
- ✔ 12 x 12-inch piece of fabric
- ✔ Ribbon
- ✔ Needle
- ✔ Thread
- ✔ Cardboard to use as pattern
- ✔ Scissors
- ✔ Ruler

1 Cut the cardboard into a triangle that's 12 x 12 x 17 inches to use as a pattern for your scarf.

2 Take your cardboard triangle and trace the outline on the back of your fabric.

3 Next, cut your scarf out of the fabric, cutting along the outline.

4 Now, just cut two 12-inch pieces of ribbon and sew one end to each corner of the 17-inch side.

5 Bingo! You've got an instant wardrobe update!

TIP: For a more finished scarf, ask an adult to help you sew a narrow hem around the edges before attaching ribbon.

Cool cuff bracelet

Wonder Woman wore them in the '70s to fight against evil — now these cool cuffs can bring you a new style power all your own! Look for inexpensive, plastic cuff bracelets at department or discount stores, then dress them up with your favorite trims for some all-out super-style action!

1 For some "budding" style, cut the flower head from the stem of a fake flower and use fabric glue to affix to your cuff — use a single large blossom or several smaller ones!

2 More cool cuffs! Starting at one end of the cuff, wind plastic or leather cording around the cuff, affixing with fabric glue as you go. Keep the rows of cording as tight as possible as you wind for an ultra-finished look.

3 For some fab furry-stuff cuffs, dab some glue on the cuff and wrap a piece of faux fur snugly around, folding under the edges. Cut slits at the corners of the fabric to get a smoother fit.

Difficulty rating ✄ ✄

2

Retro-a-go-go

Now you can turn last season's (or last decade's!) looks into the latest from today's fashion pages.

*W*ith just a few snips here, a little emphasis there, you'll have a new favorite hanging in your closet! Best yet, you can personalize it to get just the style you're looking for. The projects in this chapter require some light sewing, so make sure you get an adult to help you whether you're stitching by hand or using the machine!

Flip-flop fun

Flip-flops are all the rage — and now you can add your own flair to any ordinary pair to create these fashion musts. All for just a few pennies! And they're so easy to make, you'll soon have matching pairs for all your outfits! Flowers make for a fresh, flirty look or try tasseled trims for something more exotic.

Materials list
- ✔ 1 pair flip-flops
- ✔ Strong fabric glue
- ✔ Fabric or plastic flowers or trim
- ✔ Scissors

1 Cut the flower head from the stem as close to the base of the flower head as possible.

2 Dab a drop of glue onto the back of the flower head.

3 Place the flower in the center of the flip-flop where the straps meet and allow to dry.

Difficulty rating ✂ ✂

TIP: Instead of one big flower, you can also glue a bunch of smaller flowers all along the straps!

These were so cool and easy to make – I made pairs for my sister and myself in less than half an hour!

Talia, 11

"Vintage" cropped jeans

Say good-bye to last year's bell-bottoms and create cropped jeans with the antiqued frayed edge that are just *très* cool. (An especially groovy look when paired with your new flower flip-flops!)

Materials list
- ✔ Old jeans
- ✔ Scissors
- ✔ Sandpaper
- ✔ Ruler
- ✔ Chalk

1 Use the ruler to measure up and mark the spot where you want to cut your jeans (just above the ankle works well for sandals and boots).

2 Mark the spot with chalk. Continue measuring up the same distance around the trouser leg and marking with chalk. (This will be your guide when cutting.) Repeat with the second leg.

3 Cut straight across each trouser leg using the chalk marks as a guide to make sure the cut is even.

4 To create the frayed style, rub the cut edge of each trouser leg with sandpaper!

 TIP: For a totally trendy look, cut off the waistband on your jeans — and fray with sandpaper as well!

I always thought you had to wash your jeans a hundred times to get that worn look. The sandpaper trick was cool!

Rianne, 10

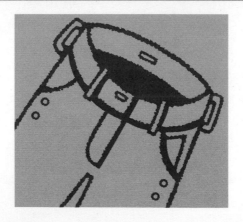

Denim & ribbon redo

Here's another great way to save an old pair of jeans, while adding some extra style! Check out fabric shops for fun ribbon and trim patterns.

Materials list
- ✔ Old denim jeans
- ✔ 40 inches ribbon or trim
- ✔ Scissors
- ✔ Thread
- ✔ Pins

1 Wrap the ribbon along the bottom cuff of the jeans, placing the bottom edge of the ribbon along the bottom edge of the cuff.

2 Pin the ribbon in place and cut off the excess.

3 Using a sewing machine, sew the top and bottom edges of the ribbon to the cuff.

4 Repeat on the other leg for a whole new look!

> **TIP:** You can try adding an extra row of ribbon (try another pattern!) an inch or so above the cuff trim, on the waistband, or on the top of the pockets for some added flair!

Studded duds

ADULT HELP NEEDED!

Looking to add some rock star glamour to your wardrobe? Shiny metal studs are the way to hit the top of the style charts! You can add them to the bottom of capris and shorts — or create your own studded designs on T-shirts, tank tops — whatever! Big hint: The thinner the fabric, the easier it is to work the studs. You can find studs at craft or fabric shops.

Materials list
- ✔ T-shirt, capris, tank top, etc.
- ✔ Metal studs (silver or gold)
- ✔ Hammer

1 Start by marking with a pencil where you want to put the studs. Try lining the bottom of each trouser leg, pockets, or create your own free-floating design — hearts, stars, your initials — whatever!

2 Push the prongs of the stud through the fabric — be careful not to hurt your fingers when it comes through the other side!

3 After the prong has been fully inserted, turn the clothing item inside out and get an adult to flatten out the prongs using the hammer.

Now you're ready to rock the town (or maybe just your living room!).

Difficulty rating ✂ ✂ ✂

TIP: Adding studs to this next project will make it twice as groovy!

Sassy sleeveless T-neck

Updating your look with a sassy
sleeveless top couldn't be easier!
Just snip and cut your way to a
new fashion favorite with the help
of these simple instructions and a
little sewing savvy.

Materials list
✔ Long-sleeved turtleneck
   shirt (make sure not to use
   a knitted sweater, as it can
   easily unravel)
✔ Scissors
✔ Needle
✔ Thread
✔ Iron
✔ Ruler
✔ Chalk
✔ Sewing machine

❶ Use the ruler to measure out ½ inch from the
seam where the sleeve meets the body of the
shirt. Mark this spot with the chalk. Continue
marking a ½ inch out from the seam all around
(front and back). Repeat with other sleeve.

2 Carefully cut off the sleeve along the ½-inch marks.

3 Now, fold the ½-inch flap down from the seam inside the shirt to create a hem.

4 Press with an iron to keep the flap down — be careful, we don't want any burned fingers! Definitely get an adult to help with this part!

5 Sew the hem by hand or with a machine. Again, if you're not completely secure in your sewing skills, a grown-up might come in handy at this point!

Difficulty rating ✂ ✂ ✂

There you go — instant wardrobe update!

Beaded T

More sparkling fun with a funky beaded top!
Choose your pattern, draw it on, and start
sewing your way to bead-a-rific style!

Materials list

- ✔ Seed beads in different colors
- ✔ T-shirt
- ✔ Needle
- ✔ Thread
- ✔ Pencil

1 Using the pencil, sketch a pattern on your
T-shirt that you'd like to use for your design.
Flowers, hearts, stars — simple designs work
best!

2 Thread your needle and knot the end. Pull the
needle through from the inside of the T-shirt out
onto the design.

3 Add a bead and pull the needle back
through to the inside of the T-shirt.

4 Repeat steps 3 and 4 — working around the design and adding your choice of different-colored beads.

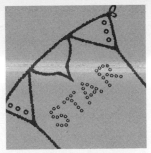

5 After you pull the last bead through, tie off the thread with a knot to secure it.

Voilà! A *très* cool and customized look for next to nothing!

Difficulty rating ✂ ✂ ✂ ✂

TIP: Be careful to hand-wash your top to make sure your new beaded design remains fully intact!

5 *fab ways* TO WEAR A *feather boa!*

There's nothing quite so glammy as a fluffy feather boa. Sure, sporting one solo on your next trip to the mall might be a little over the top, but there's nothing better when it comes to an easy and fun way to update your oh-so-

blah basics. If you don't happen to have one hanging around your house (left over from a long-gone Halloween?), you can pick one up pretty inexpensively at craft or party shops.

1 Turn a basic shirt or sweater into a fun and fluffy party top! By sewing simple feather boa accents around the neck and sleeves, you'll make the ordinary EXTRA-ordinary! You'll find this project works best on tops with a simple round neckline.

2 Spice up the bottom of an old skirt (don't forget those vintage or secondhand shops!) by sewing a feather boa along the hemline. Talk about adding some swing to your style. So, so groovy!

3 Looking to liven up your capris? Add some fun to your summer style by sewing a length of feather boa around the bottom of each leg! Bright, tropical colors on white capris are soooo French Riviera!

4 Trim the top and sleeves of last season's jean jacket with the boa of your choice — what could be more fun?

5 Viva Las Vegas! Not quite ready to go out of the house with your new feathered friend? Try trimming robes and slippers with a bit of boa. Then host a sleepover party to show off your glamorous new sleepwear!

TIP: Make sure you hand-wash your new hip creations — you don't want your feathers to start molting!

Difficulty rating ✂ ✂ ✂

MORE FUN AND FUNKY
DIY *style tricks!*

 Military badges are all the rage. Create your own salute to   military style by picking up authentic badges at your local army and navy store. Sew on jean pockets and T-shirt sleeves. And while you're there, pick up a canvas camouflage army belt — too cool!

Big hair, off-the-shoulder shirts — the '80s are back (just stay away from the oversized shoulder pads à la *Dynasty*). Instead, think vintage Madonna and get stuck on the latest safety-pin craze.

Make slits up the sides of your jeans (on the seams) and pin them back together (style doesn't necessarily have to make sense!).

Stick it to your shirts! Try the same trick on your sleeves, by cutting up the seam from the cuff to the elbow and pinning back together. Or, create the off-the-shoulder look by cutting off the neckband of an old T and adding a few pins on the shoulder seams!

DIY*style*

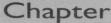Chapter

Divine
Decorating

Say good-bye to that oh-so-blah bedroom and hello to adding some major personal style!

$\mathcal{W}$hether your room's in need of a major makeover or just a mini face-lift, in this chapter you'll find some divine decorating ideas sure to add some personality with just a few easy steps! Just make sure you get Mom's OK before doing any big-time "renovations"!

A LITTLE *something about* COLOR

One of the best things you can do to update your room is give it a fresh coat of paint. But when it comes to color choices, which way should you go? Other than simply choosing a color you like, some people believe that the colors you choose to surround yourself with actually influence your emotions — and even your health!

Try conducting a little experiment of your own by walking into rooms painted in different colors — and then seeing how you feel. When you're done, check out our color chart below to see if your reaction corresponds to each color's supposed effect!

YELLOW

Believe it or not, yellow might make you smarter! Yellow is thought to promote mental stimulation and help you think quicker! So if you want your studying to pay off, you might start cramming in a yellow room. (Heck, while you're at it, throw on some Mozart and you could be acing exams left and right!)

PINK

Don't have any rose-colored glasses? Try painting your room pink . . . and you may have an improved outlook on the world around you (or at least an improved outlook on your bedroom!).

BLUES, GREENS, AND PURPLES

These are the most popular of all bedroom colors, probably because of their cool, calming effects. Always up counting sheep? Try sleeping in a room painted in one of these colors to catch the most zzzzzs.

WHITE

In desperate need of organization? White is the color of purity and said to have a cleansing

and purifying effect. (Maybe you'll actually enjoy cleaning your room?)

RED

Ever hear that expression "I'm seeing red"? Too much red is said to make people angry and agitated. Probably not a good bedroom choice.

BLACK

OK, that's just plain weird.

Enjoy "coloring your world" — or at least your room! And keep these color tricks in mind as you set out to customize your room with the projects in this chapter.

Pillow magic

Now you can make a custom pillow that's as groovy as it is easy to make! Choose fabrics that fit the style of your room. Fake leopard, fuzzy faux fur, sophisticated stripes — your choice! Not so handy with the sewing machine? Ask an adult for some help!

Materials list

- ✔ Pillow stuffing
- ✔ 30 inches fake-fur fabric
- ✔ Sewing machine
- ✔ Needle
- ✔ Thread
- ✔ Scissors
- ✔ Ruler

1 Measure and cut out two equal-sized squares of the fabric. (Be sure to make the squares roughly a ½ inch larger than the size you want the actual pillow to be.)

2 Next, place the two pieces together with the front of the fabric facing inside.

3 Sew the pieces together around all four sides, stitching about a ¼ inch in from the edge. Leave 2 inches unsewn at the end, to insert the stuffing.

4 Turn the pillow right side out — and stuff in the stuffing!

5 Now simply sew the opening shut and curl up and enjoy!

Tip: Try making your pillows in different shapes — hearts and circles are easy to do and look fab! To create a heart pattern, fold a large piece of paper in two and draw half of a heart starting at the fold. Cut out to create a symmetrical heart pattern that you can trace on the back of the fabric!

Beaded curtain

This fun update on those psychedelic hanging beads from the '60s will make any room so, so groovy! However, we recommend actually hanging this one across your window rather than your door!

ADULT HELP NEEDED!

Materials list
✔ Large- and medium-sized beads of different shapes and colors
✔ A dowel or curtain rod long enough to fit across your window
✔ String
✔ Scissors

1 Cut between fifteen to twenty 40-inch lengths of string.

2 Tie one end of the string around the end of the dowel or rod.

3 Slide a bead onto the string about 1 ½ inches from the rod and tie a knot under the bead to hold it in place.

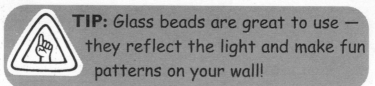

4 Slide on another bead about 1 ½ inches down and tie another knot. Continue with as many beads as you like.

5 Repeat steps 2 through 4 with the other strings.

6 Rest the rod on curtain brackets to hang your new beaded creation!

TIP: Glass beads are great to use — they reflect the light and make fun patterns on your wall!

Difficulty rating ✂ ✂

Bead-dazzling lamp shade

Turn an ordinary lamp shade from blah to bead-dazzling — and let your own sense of style shine through! All in three easy steps!

Materials list
✔ Plain fabric lamp shade
✔ White glue
✔ A few packs of seed beads in different colors

1 Draw a design on the lamp shade with the glue — swirls, hearts, flowers — you name it!

2 Sprinkle beads of one color on the glue and allow to dry.

3 Repeat with another design using a different color — and see your lamp in a whole new light!

Difficulty rating ✂ ✂

 TIP: Only work one design at a time so the glue doesn't dry out!

Fab "fur" phone

"Ring" in a funky new look using an ordinary phone and a little faux fur!

ADULT HELP NEEDED!

Materials list
- ✔ Inexpensive "cradle" phone
- ✔ 10 inches fake fur that has some "stretch" to it
- ✔ Double-sided tape
- ✔ Sharp scissors
- ✔ Ruler

1 Cut pieces of double-sided tape and apply so it completely covers the phone and base except for the cord, buttons, phone rest, and sound holes.

2 Cut the fabric in half. Wrap one half of the fabric around the top of the phone, stretching as you go and molding the fabric around the phone. Trim off any excess fur with the scissors as you go. (You may have to fill in certain areas with smaller pieces of fur afterward. Just measure the size of the space and cut the fur to fit. The fur will all blend together!)

DIY*style*

3 Repeat step 2 with the bottom of the base.

4 Cut out the areas for the sound holes, a square for the buttons and the phone.

Now you've got a furry phone that just "calls" out fun!

Decorative drawer knobs

Tired of that boring old bureau? Ready to say good night to your not-so-fab nightstand? Now you can update your furniture with decorative hand-made knobs — hand-made by you with colored polymer clay found at craft stores.

ADULT HELP NEEDED!

Materials list
✔ Polymer clay in different colors
✔ Round wooden screw-on dresser knobs
✔ Small heat-resistant beads
✔ Permanent colored markers

1 Work the different-colored pieces of clay until they're soft.

2 Use one color as a base color and form into a flat pancake approximately ¾-inch thick and long enough to fit around the knob.

3 Use your creativity to make patterns on the flattened piece with the other colors of clay. Try overlaying stripes, dots, swirls, whatever you choose!

4 Wrap the piece around the wooden knob. Now you can add any kind of beads for some extra pizzazz.

5 Bake the decorative knobs according to the clay manufacturer's directions. Once they're cool, you can further decorate with markers and attach to your dresser.

Difficulty rating ✂ ✂

TIP: Try creating different decorative knobs for each drawer!

I painted my old dresser, then added some homemade clay knobs with stars and hearts on them – I can't believe how cool it looked afterward!

Lauren, 11

Cool canopy bed

ADULT HELP NEEDED!

For you more ambitious young decorators, here's a way to add an ultra-elegant canopy to your bed without having to buy all new furniture. Believe it or not, all you need is a few plastic or metal towel rings (available in hardware or bath speciality stores), some curtains, and a little help from Mom or Dad!

Materials list
- ✔ 5 plastic or metal towel rings
- ✔ 1 large screw-in "J" hook
- ✔ 4 sheer curtain panels

1 OK, here's where the help part from Mom or Dad comes in. You need to center the towel ring in the ceiling above your bed. If you don't have a light fixture to attach the ring to, you'll

need to screw a hook into the ceiling (available from a hardware store).

2 Fold one end of one of the curtain panels around one of the towel rings so it overlaps approximately 2 inches. Sew the end of the curtain to the rest of the curtain to attach it to the ring. Repeat with the other 3 panels. Now hang the ring above your bed.

3 Now attach one ring to each of the four corners of your bed by hanging one around each bedpost. *

4 Loop the loose end of each curtain through one of the rings at each bed corner for beauteous bedroom chic!

If you don't have bedposts, you can loop the curtain panels through the ring above the ceiling and tuck the ends between the mattress and box-spring on all four corners.

Difficulty rating ✄ ✄ ✄ ✄

Flower-power light string

Add some flower power to ordinary holiday lights for a beautiful, blooming bedroom decor!

Materials list
- ✔ String of small white or colored holiday lights
- ✔ Fabric or plastic flowers (make sure they're nonflammable!)
- ✔ Strong fabric glue
- ✔ Scissors

1 Cut the flower heads from the stems as close to the base as possible.

2 Remove the center portion of the flower head so an individual bulb can fit through.

3 Apply a dab of glue to the inside of the base of the flower head and fit over the base of the bulb.

4 Drape your finished flower string across the top of curtain rod or around your bedroom door.

Difficulty rating ✂ ✂

Custom corkboard

ADULT HELP NEEDED!

Whether you're looking to totally organize your life or need a place to post your favorite mementos (like that ticket stub from your first date with your beau!), a bulletin board is totally indispensable to preteen life. Now you can make a cool custom version from ordinary corkboard purchased at lumberyards or office supply stores!

Materials list
- Corkboard
- Fabric (large enough to wrap around corkboard)
- Thumbtacks
- Ribbon
- Upholsterer's tacks (optional)
- Small adhesive hooks

1 Measure the dimensions of the corkboard and cut a fabric piece slightly larger all the way around.

2 Wrap the fabric snugly around the cork-board and secure to the back of the corkboard with thumbtacks. (If it's a little messy, don't worry, no one will see the back!)

3 Cut lengths of ribbon large enough to fit around the corkboard and arrange in a pattern across your corkboard. You can create a simple grid pattern, randomly crisscross diagonally across the board — whatever! Secure each end of the ribbon to the back of the corkboard with the thumbtacks.

4 Secure each point where the ribbons cross with a thumbtack or upholsterer's tack (similar to a thumbtack — usually just prettier!) to make sure your lists, postcards, ticket stubs, etc. don't fall out.

5 Stick the two adhesive hooks on either end of the corkboard. Tie a piece of ribbon to both hooks and tie together in a bow and hang from a nail.

6 Slip your favorite mementos underneath

the ribbon for a totally custom keepsake corkboard!

MORE *fun* USES FOR A *feather boa*

You can also add some
feathers to your nest with
these fun and funky deco-
rating ideas using an inexpensive boa!

 Arm yourself with
fabric glue and stick a
length of boa around
the top and bottom of a basic lamp shade to
add some major groove and to totally turn
on the style! Make sure to glue it in sections so the glue doesn't dry before you
secure the boa.

 Has your old mirror seen better days? Have
a frame in desperate need of some funk?

Grab that fabric glue again and affix a feather boa to the outside edge. Make sure that you glue the center piece that holds the feathers rather than just the ends of the feathers. Trim off any excess boa and you're done!

Add some sass to those drab curtains! Stitch a length of feather boa to the bottom and top edges — so, so groovy!

Tickle your fancy with more pillow fun! Perk up an ordinary pillow by stitching some boa along the outside edge!

ANCIENT Feng Shui SECRETS!

Could the placement of your bed be creating chaos in your life? Does the color of your carpet promote positive energy? Feng Shui says it can. Feng Shui is the ancient Eastern art of living in harmony with your surroundings. It includes some quirky rules for setting up your home to best promote the movement of "chi" — or energy — around you. So, now that you've added some personal groove to your room, make sure that the chi is flowing (after all, there's nothing worse than blocked chi!).

Here are a few Feng Shui tips to keep in mind when organizing your room:

Be sure to place the head of your bed against a wall — this will promote protection and stability.

Place the bed so that you have clear sight of the door. The idea is that you should be able to clearly see who's entering the room, but without being in the path of incoming energy.

Go for enclosed bookcases rather than open shelves to avoid negative energy shooting out at you!

Plants increase luck — even fake plants, so have plenty around.

A messy or disorganized room can lead to disharmony. Try to keep those clothes in the closet and off your floor! (Mom and Dad will love this one!)

Place taller items like dressers or vases to the left of the bed to increase wisdom. (Imagine if you tried this, painted your room yellow, AND listened to Mozart? Watch out, Einstein!)

PART 2

LIFE-"*Style*"

*S*tyle isn't just about clothing and decorating. Even the little things we do and use on a day-to-day basis reflect our own individual sense of style. The types of soaps you choose, the smell of a favorite perfume, the gifts you decide to give to people — even the types of gatherings you throw – are all personal choices that express who you are! In this section, you'll get some ideas on how to surround yourself (and others!) with some fun life-"style" extras! Just be careful that no one is allergic to the ingredients in the gifts you make or it will be bye-bye to all that time and effort.

DIY*style*

Chapter 4

Lotions & Potions

Oooh, sweet-smelling soaps, luscious lip balms, luxurious lotions that soothe, protect, and soften the skin – who doesn't love them?

$\mathcal{B}$ut one visit to those fancy gift shops and bath and beauty boutiques and you might as well say good-bye to your pocket money for the next two months.

In this chapter, you'll find out how to create scrumptious body lotions and potions that are all the rage, using the same quality ingredients and techniques as the pros. Plus some fun packaging ideas to make your creation perfectly complete. And the fragrance, shapes, and colors you choose to put in your fabulous concoctions all say something about YOU!

ESSENTIAL INFO
on essential oils

Essential oils from spearmint, lavender, lemon, and tons of other sweet- (and not-so-sweet-) smelling plants have been used for hundreds and hundreds of years to naturally scent everything from perfumes and bath and body products to housecleaning supplies (hmmm, not quite so glamorous!). So what's the deal with essential oils? Well, they are the aromatic extracts collected from plants through a variety of different processes, depending on the type of plant. Steam distillation, cold pressing, and solvent extractions are just a few of the methods commonly used to gather oils today. These extracts can come from many different parts of the plant. For example, lemon, orange, and grapefruit oils, also called citrus oils, come from the peel of the fruit, but extracts can also come from the flower, bark, root, leaves, berries, and seeds of other plants.

With all the hoopla around essential oils and aromatherapy (the use of plant fragrances for the healing of body, mind, and spirit) you'd think it might just be a new style "trend." But in reality, the ancient Egyptians first began using essential oils in cosmetics as far back as 3000 BC — not only because they smelled great, but because they thought the oils would help them stay young and beautiful. Today, essential oils are used in everything from perfume and soaps to massage and medicine.

Here's a list of popular and easy-to-find oils and their properties (all should be available at health food stores). Feel free to experiment with your favorite oils by substituting them in the lotions and potions recipes that follow!

TIP: These extracts are superstrong and super-concentrated and should be used very carefully. Never apply essential oils directly to the skin — they should always be diluted and mixed before using!

CHAMOMILE — Having a tough time falling asleep? Have a cup of chamomile tea to help wind the system down!

LAVENDER — Nervous about that big test? Had a tough day at school? Lavender oil is said to have a calming effect on the senses. Add a few drops to your bath to help you completely de-stress.

LEMON — Feeling a little sluggish? Have to clear some cobwebs? The light, clean scent of lemon oil is noted for being energizing as well as mentally stimulating.

ORANGE — Need to "center yourself" before a big game or first date? Orange oil has a relaxing while at the same time uplifting effect, so you don't start snoozing halfway through!

PEPPERMINT — Looking for a little pick-me-up after a late-night sleepover? Stay away from the caffeine and take a few whiffs of peppermint's refreshing and invigorating scent instead!

ROSEMARY — Could you use an extra boost of mental power? People claim to experience increased mental clarity and improved memory after inhaling just a few drops of the oil.

TEA TREE — While not the sweetest-smelling oil, tea tree has gained big popularity for its strong antiseptic qualities. Tea tree is one of the few oils that can be directly applied to the skin and is commonly used to treat cuts, sunburn, and even that occasional zit!

DIY*style*

"Peppy"-mint cleansing bar

For the gal on the go, this refreshing
bar promises to add a little oomph
to your day from the very first lather! Plus, you can use cookie cutters
to cut your soap into custom shapes
that make it oh-so-fun to use. Best yet, it can
all be done in the microwave! What could be
simpler?

Materials list
- ✔ Peppermint essential oil (found
  at health food stores)
- ✔ Glycerine-based soap (found at
  pharmacies or craft shops)
- ✔ Cookie cutters
- ✔ Grater
- ✔ Microwave-safe container
- ✔ Plate (the plate should be
  slightly deeper in the center)
- ✔ Ladle

1 Use the grater to grate the glycerine soap
into the microwave-safe container. Heat on
high until the soap is completely melted

(the time depends on your microwave). Keep checking at 15-second intervals.

2 While the soap is melting, place a few drops (two or three) of the essential oil onto a plate and spread around.

3 Carefully pour the melted glycerine onto the plate, making sure it's at least ¾-inch thick. Allow the soap to cool and harden.

4 Once the soap has cooled, push your cookie cutter(s) into it to create your individual bars. Remember to save the leftovers for future soap projects!

5 Using a damp cloth, smooth out any rough edges . . . and lather up!

Difficulty rating ✂ ✂ ✂

DIY*style*

TIP: Here's a tip to add some EXTRA style to your soap! Try using a heart-shaped cookie cutter and pressing little heart-shaped beads into the soap immediately after pouring it onto the plate. When the soap cools, the hearts will be floating inside!

I LOVE the way this soap smells! I made a bunch in the shapes of angels and Christmas trees, then wrapped them in green tissue paper and ribbon – they were great stocking-stuffers for my mom and sister!

Cecilia, 10

Chunky soap cubes

ADULT HELP NEEDED!

You don't need to invest in lots of expensive equipment to make your own custom soap creations. This project shows how ordinary household objects like ice-cube trays can make super soap molds! (Just make sure no one tries to put one of your soap cubes in a tall glass of Coke!)

Materials list

- ✔ Ice-cube tray
- ✔ Liquid food coloring
- ✔ Glycerine soap
- ✔ Petroleum jelly
- ✔ Cotton swabs or toothpick
- ✔ Microwave-safe container
- ✔ Grater

1 Use the grater to grate the glycerine soap into a microwave-safe container.

2 Using a cotton swab or toothpick, dab a tiny bit of the liquid food coloring (you only need a little) into the container as well.

3 Next, use a cotton swab to coat the inside of the ice-cube tray with petroleum jelly (so the soap doesn't stick!).

4 Pour the melted glycerine into the ice-cube trays, filling up as many of the sections as you can.

5 Allow to cool for about 2 hours (you don't have to put them in the freezer!).

6 Once cooled, the soap cubes should pop right out!

Difficulty rating ✂ ✂ ✂

TIP: Try doing a few batches, each in a different color, and display in a clear glass bowl, or package in a clear plastic bag with glittery ribbon.

Refreshing citrus scent

Materials list
- ✔ 1 teaspoon lemon oil
- ✔ 1 tablespoon mandarin oil
- ✔ 3 cups ethyl alcohol (available at pharmacies)

1 Mix the mandarin oil with 1 cup of the alcohol until blended. Add the remaining alcohol and stir.

2 Stir in the lemon oil.

3 Store in an airtight container for 4 to 6 weeks for it to reach its scentsational peak!

TIP: This flirty fragrance also makes a great gift when packaged in a delicate container and tied with a ribbon. For an extra-personalized touch, add your own "designer" tag!

This was so easy and smells awesome! The hardest part was having to wait.

Alyssa, 9

Luscious lip balm

Now you can create your own yummy lip balm in the comfort of your own kitchen! The flavored oils used in this recipe can be found at a kitchen supply store or a craft store with a candy-making department. Try any one of your fave

flavors — raspberry, strawberry, banana, or all three together! This recipe calls for a stove — make sure an adult is around to supervise!

Materials list
- ✔ 4 teaspoons beeswax
- ✔ 6 teaspoons sunflower oil
- ✔ 5-6 drops flavored oil
- ✔ Small saucepan
- ✔ Aluminum measuring cup
- ✔ Metal spoon
- ✔ Scissors
- ✔ Small containers to hold lip balm

1 Fill the saucepan halfway with water.

2 Pour the sunflower oil into the measuring cup and place inside the saucepan. Turn the heat on low and gently warm the oil.

3 Slowly add the beeswax to the warm oil inside the measuring cup. Wait for the beeswax to melt. (As the beeswax is melting, make sure there's enough water in the saucepan . . . or that it doesn't overflow. Have an adult help you pour out the water if there's too much, or add more if there's too little!)

4 Once the beeswax has melted, use the metal spoon to thoroughly mix together the oil and beeswax.

5 Add the flavored oil and stir again to blend.

6 Turn off the heat and remove the aluminum measuring cup from the saucepan (make sure to use oven gloves — the aluminum will be hot!).

7 While still warm, spoon or pour the balm into containers and set aside for 20 minutes before covering.

Difficulty rating ✄ ✄ ✄ ✄

All-that-glitters gel

Not only is our glitter gel at the height of fashion, it's good for your skin, too! Make sure you use glitter designated for "cosmetic use"!

Materials list
- ✔ 1/4 teaspoon fine polyester glitter
- ✔ 1/4 cup aloe vera gel
- ✔ 1 teaspoon glycerine
- ✔ Containers for your glitter

1 Mix the aloe and glycerine in a small bowl.

2 Stir in the glitter until well mixed and spoon into containers.

Difficulty rating ✂

Bath bomb

Add one of these homemade bath bombs to your bath and watch it "explode" with super skin-softening ingredients.

Materials list
- ✔ 3 tablespoons coconut oil (almond oil or avocado oil will also work!)
- ✔ Liquid food coloring
- ✔ 4 to 5 drops of your favorite essential oil
- ✔ 2 ounces baking powder
- ✔ 2 tablespoons cornstarch
- ✔ 2 tablespoons citric acid
- ✔ Waxed paper

1 Place all of the dry ingredients into a bowl and mix well.

2 Mix the fragrance and coloring together.

3 In a small glass bowl, combine the oil with the fragrance and coloring mixture.

4 Slowly add the oil mixture to the dry ingredients and blend well.

5 Take spoon-sized scoops of the mixture and shape into balls. The balls should be about three-quarters of an inch in diameter. Let the balls rest on a sheet of waxed paper for 2 to 3 hours.

6 The bombs must dry and harden for 1 to 2 days. (I know it's hard to wait!)

7 To use, drop one to three bombs into the bath and watch it fizzzzzz!

Vanilla swirl bubble bath

Swirl together your favorite fruit and vanilla scents to create a yummy bubble bath that smells good enough to eat! You may never leave the tub again!

Materials list

- ✔ 1¹/₄ cups unscented liquid soap
- ✔ 6³/₄ tablespoons distilled water (available at supermarkets)
- ✔ 8 drops vanilla fragrance oil
- ✔ 6 drops fruit-scented fragrance oil
- ✔ 2 drops food coloring — red or blue makes for some "berry" good color!

Mix all the ingredients together in a bowl, pour into containers — and bingo! Instant bubble-licious bubble bath!

Difficulty rating ✂

Soothing eye pillow

Zone out after a long day with this totally relaxing treat for your eyes. Try using a light cotton fabric and dried herbs available at health food stores for the best results.

ADULT HELP NEEDED!

Materials list
- ✓ Approximately 12 x 8-inch piece of fabric
- ✓ A few handfuls of dried herbs
- ✓ Needle
- ✓ Thread

1 Cut the fabric into two 12 x 4-inch pieces and place them together with the front sides of the pieces facing each other.

2 Sew them together using a sewing machine — or hand-stitch with a needle and thread, leaving a gap of approximately 2 inches unsewn.

3 Turn the fabric right side out and stuff with herbs. To make the filling process easier, make a cone with a sheet of paper, putting the small end inside the fabric and fill from the opposite end.

4 Once filled (don't be afraid to overstuff!), sew the gap closed. Hit the couch, place the pillow over your eyes and . . . zzzzz!

TIP: Be sure to store your finished eye pillow in the fridge for some extra-soothing relief!

Smoothing body scrub

Try buying a salt scrub at your favorite bath shop and you'll have to shell out tons of money. Now you can get the same results at a smidgen of the price!

Materials list
- ✔ 1/2 cup coarse sea salt
- ✔ 3/4 cup mineral oil
- ✔ 2-3 drops of your favorite essential oil
- ✔ Bowl
- ✔ Fork
- ✔ Glass containers

Pour the above into a bowl — and mix. That's it!

Difficulty rating ✂

TIP: Clean out glass baby food or peanut butter jars to hold your scrub!

This is just like the scrub my mom buys at the store — except I made it!

Rachel, 9

Gifty Goodies

"Handmade" doesn't have to mean the 1970s macramé plant hanger hanging in your great-aunt's house!

$\mathcal{I}$n this chapter, you'll find directions for oh-so-stylish gifts perfect for friends, families — anyone — all handmade with that little something extra by y-o-u! Plus check out cool alternatives to traditional (yawn!) gift wrap and cards sure to complete your totally personalized package. So next time you're looking for the perfect gift, look around the house for some materials and make it! But watch out, you might make gifts so fab, you'll want to keep them for yourself!

Lavender mini pillows

Lavender has often been used in sachets to scent clothes drawers — but these potpourri goodies are so adorable you'll almost hate to hide them! Check out the remnants section at a fabric store for small pieces of material at great prices. And be sure to ask an adult for a little help if you're not 100 percent handy with a needle and thread or sewing machine.

1 Cut two pieces of fabric the same size. 4½ x 4½ inches makes a good size for a sachet, but you can choose whatever size works for you!

2 Sew the two pieces together (on a machine or by hand). The sides that you want showing on the outside of the pillow should be facing each other when you sew the pieces together. Make sure to leave a 2-inch opening on one side to put the lavender in!

3 Turn right side out, fill with lavender, and stitch the opening closed.

TIP: For a fun look, choose two different fabrics for the same pillow! Or try sewing a large bead to each corner.

Difficulty rating ✂ ✂ ✂

Totally custom journal

A journal or photo album is a pretty personal thing, so why not give one that says something about the person you're making it for? There are tons of ways to decorate a journal, but here are a few ideas to get you started.

Materials list
✔ Ribbon
✔ Strong fabric glue
✔ Glue stick
✔ Acrylic paint
✔ Blank notepad with spiral spine (at craft and stationery stores, you can find nice sturdy versions of these, often used for scrapbooks)
✔ Decorative materials like beads, silk flowers, postcards, photos

1 You can add some extra dimension to your journal or album by painting the cover. Make sure to protect the inside pages by placing newspaper over them while you paint. The plain cardboard look is also cool for a more earthy-type cover.

2 Once the paint is dry, it's time to add the extras. Here are a few ideas:

Looking to find a gift for a travel buff? Decorate the cover with a single old postcard. Glue it to the front of the pad using the glue stick. For a more finished look, try lining the outside edge of the postcard with ribbon. Just cut lengths of ribbon the same length as the postcard edge and stick down with a few dabs of the fabric glue.

Pick up a few fabric flowers and cut the flower head from the stem. Stick the flower heads to the cover of the album using the fabric glue.

Create a monogram with beads! Trace initials on the cover. Next, string beads on a piece of thread — make sure the string is roughly the same length as the first initial —

and knot the end. Trace the initial with the fabric glue (you need a steady hand for this one, so ask an adult for help if you need to!). Lay the string of beads over the glue and hold down. Repeat for the other initials.

Even more fun with fur! Cut out some fun shapes from pieces of faux fur — and glue on the front, or cover the whole thing in fur, fur, fully fab fur!

TIP: To turn your journal into a photo album, glue in photo corners (also available at craft stores) to hold your fave pics!

Difficulty rating ✂ ✂

"Fab"-ric vase

Always giving Mom flowers for her birthday? Mother's Day? Why not make the bouquet say something extra with a fab fabric vase? Fabric remnants work great here, too.

1 Measure the height and width around the container.

2 Cut a piece of fabric ¼ inch taller and wider than the height and width of the container.

3 Apply glue to the bottom and two ends of the fabric piece, leaving the top unglued. Line up the bottom edge of the fabric with the bottom of the container and wrap it around tightly. Press down firmly along the edges!

4 Glue the underside of the fabric that remains at the top and fold the edges inside the vase. Try cutting a few slits in the fabric from the edge to the point where it meets the container to make folds neater.

5 Try adding a little extra personality with some ribbon or trim!

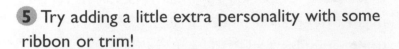

Difficulty rating ✂ ✂

I made a vase with this really pretty striped material and my mom buys flowers special just to put in it!

Jennifer, 10

Origami gift box

Who said origami was all about
making paper cranes? (Which, by
the way, can make for a great mobile
when tied with different lengths of string to a
hanger!) You can use this ancient art of paper
folding to make a fun and funky little container
that's great for packaging small gifts. Or you
might even decide to use it as a gift itself! Try
using wrapping paper for a more delicate box,
or heavier handmade paper for something a
little more sturdy.

ADULT HELP NEEDED!

Materials list
- ✔ 7 x 7-inch square of
  paper (for lid)
- ✔ 6½ x 6½-inch square
  of paper (for bottom)
- ✔ Ruler
- ✔ Pencil
- ✔ Glue stick
- ✔ Scissors

1 Place the 7 x 7-inch paper for the lid
facedown. Lay the ruler diagonally across the

paper and draw a line to the opposite corners.
Repeat with the other two corners so you
have a perfect "X" going across the sheet.

2 Fold one corner to the center of the "X"
and unfold. (Now here's where it gets tricky!)
Fold the same corner up to the crease made in
the previous fold. Keep the corner in this folded position and fold the paper along the original crease. Then fold it once more so that it
touches the center line.

3 Unfold and repeat the steps 1 and 2 above
for the other three corners.

4 Pick a corner and cut slits down the folds to
the right and left of the center line. Cut until you
reach the outside edge of the middle square created by the fold. You should finish one block
away from the center of the paper.

5 Repeat on opposite corner.

6 Fold down just the pointed
top of one of the wider triangle-
shaped sides. Fold over again,
then fold the triangular tabs at either

end in to make a "U" shape. Stand this up to make it one side of your box.

7 Repeat step 6 with opposite side.

8 To make the box shape, fold over the pointed tip of one of the remaining two sides. Then fold up and over the tabs created in steps 5–6.

9 Repeat with opposite side. Glue the sides down with a glue stick to keep the box shape.

10 To make the lid, repeat steps 1 to 9 with the smaller piece of paper. Be patient, practice makes a perfect box!

Difficulty rating ✂ ✂ ✂ ✂

Gifty BASKETS

A tisket a tasket, what could be more fun than a customized gift basket — especially one filled with fun theme-based presents? With a little creativity, you can make a one-of-a-kind "basket" especially tailored to the interests of the lucky recipient. Check out these theme basket ideas, or use a little creative thinking to come up with some ideas of your own!

Beach tote

Here's a great gift idea for anyone heading to the shore or the pool! Perfect for that favorite beach bum in your life!

Pick up an inexpensive beach tote from a discount store, toss in some sunscreen, high SPF lip balm, self-tanning lotion, sunglasses, blooming ponytail holder, and a mag for a complete summer gift kit!

Car wash caddie

Looking for that special gift for Dad? Create this simple car wash caddie for a surefire Father's Day or birthday hit!

Start with a plastic bucket from a hardware store, add a sponge, a few polishing cloths, car wax, a car freshener, etc. Top with a bow and you're set to go!

Chef's special!

Have a cook on your gift list? Start with a large mixing bowl, add a couple gourmet gifts, and you've got the recipe for a "well-done" present! Try adding culinary extras like wooden spoons, seasonings and spices, a dishcloth, or a favorite baking recipe and its ingredients!

Beauty bag

Create a mini-makeover in a bag! Your gal pals will absolutely love it!

Grab an inexpensive makeup bag — or make your own drawstring bag by sewing together two pieces of fabric, and sewing a quarter-inch hem around the top — leaving a small opening for drawing a string through. (If you attach a safety pin to the end, it's easier to pull through!) Throw in some fun beauty musts like nail polish, a nail file, lip gloss — you can even include some of your homemade body glitter, lotion, smoothing body scrub, bath bombs, and a glitter hair clip!

Gardener's delight

You're sure to plant some big thanks from the gardener on your list with this thoughtful grower's gift.

Use a medium-sized terra-cotta pot to hold your gardening goodies. Include things like seeds, a box of plant food, gardener's gloves, a trowel, and hand lotion. Tie a bow around the pot to finish your gardener's bounty!

Cookie cutter gift cards

What better way to add that something extra to your gift than with an adorably designed note card? With a few simple materials and a little creativity, you can make a cute card to fully complete your package.

Materials list

✔ Thin card stock or construction paper
✔ Cookie cutters
✔ Scissors
✔ Glue stick
✔ Hole punch
✔ Marker, ribbon, buttons, pipe cleaners

1 Fold the piece of card stock or construction paper in half.

2 Line up the cookie cutter so the top is on the fold and trace around the outside of it with a pencil.

3 Cut out the design, being careful not to cut along the fold. This is where the card will open.

4 Add extra decorations to the card! Using a gingerbread cookie cutter? Glue real buttons down the middle and draw eyes with a marker. A heart-shaped cutter? Tie a bow with a ribbon and glue it on. An angel? Try creating a halo out of a pipe cleaner and attaching it with glue.

5 Use the hole punch to create a hole so you can tie string through and attach to your gift.

Difficulty rating ✂ ✂

MORE COOL
card ideas

Nothing says "I Love You" more than a home-made card! Send the very best with a one-of-a-kind greeting made from some paper and a few project leftovers.

Create a card that does double duty as a mini-gift! Use a few leftover beads and a piece of elastic to make a bead ring. Tie with a ribbon and glue the knot to the front of a card made from handmade paper.

Try the same trick with a charm and piece of ribbon to create a choker-in-a-card! Cut two small slits into the front of the card, string a charm onto a ribbon and slip the ends through the slit. Tie a loose knot to secure the ribbon inside the card and let the charm dangle from the front.

Is it a card or a journal? Fold a piece of heavy handmade paper in half. Cut a few sheets of writing paper slightly smaller than the opened handmade paper. Fold the sheets in half and line up the folds inside the handmade paper fold. Secure the inside pages by tying some elastic string (silver or gold looks cool!) around the fold. Include some favorite quotes, poems, or just leave the pages blank for that special someone to fill in!

WRAP IT UP!

In a pinch for some wrapping paper? Or maybe you're looking to add a little flair to your gift packages? Here are some ideas to make your gift something extra-special — even before it gets opened!

Try using an old map as wrapping paper on gifts for your favorite traveler.

Use handmade paper in place of traditional wrap for some extra elegance.

Wrap your gift in plain white paper, then wrap over the paper with colored plastic wrap from your kitchen drawer.

 Rummage through your fabric remnants to create some high-style gift wrap.

 Use brown paper and a rubber stamp (or make your own stamp by cutting out a shape on a raw potato!) of your favorite designs for a totally custom wrap.

Bows, bows, bows!

Try using fabric ribbon, raffia, or silk flowers in place of traditional bows for even more super style!

When I'm totally stuck for wrapping paper, I just hit the kitchen and use some aluminium foil!

Brigitte, 11

Chapter

6

Entertaining

As any great hostess knows, the real secret of entertaining, and the number one prerequisite for a successful party is — of course — **STYLE**!

Introduction

Sure, anyone can serve up a pizza and some drinks for friends, but entertaining is really about making the gathering a total "experience" for everyone involved. And this is where your personal style comes into play.

If you think about it, everything from your choice of invitations to the food, music, and party favors says something about you and your style. In this chapter, you'll learn the ins and outs of throwing a great party (or just a simple get-together), find loads of entertaining tips, decorating ideas, themes, and some whimsical recipes that are fun to make and even more fun to eat — yummm! (Just be sure to ALWAYS, ALWAYS have an adult around when you get ready to start cookin'!) Best yet, you'll be able to put to use some of the lessons you've already learned in this book. Watch out, Martha Stewart!

When it comes to entertaining, just like anything else, there are some rules you need to live (and plan) by to assure true party success. But don't worry — once you get them down, your shindigs will be the most sought-after social events in town!

WHAT TYPE OF EVENT?

First things first. When it comes to planning any kind of get-together, the first priority is to establish what kind of event you're going after.

Are you looking to host an all-out bash, or would you rather an intimate little soiree for your best girlfriends? A lot of this depends on your personality (do you like being around a lot of people, or are you more comfortable with just a few friends?).

Resources like space, money, and available help (can you bribe your younger brother?) are also a huge determining factor. (Do I have the room to have a bunch of people over? How much is it going to cost? And how long will it take me to prepare — and clean up?!)

Of course, it goes without saying that the 'rents need to be included in all your grand planning — make sure you get their OK before you even start thinking "party"!

Creating the guest list

Once you've determined what kind of event you're going for, the next step is to create the guest list.

In terms of numbers of people, a general rule of thumb is to invite 20 percent more people than the actual number you'd like to attend — figure that a few people here and there won't be able to make it (but will totally regret it after they hear about it!).

For those math-challenged hostesses, this means that if you want 10 people to show up, invite 12. If you're looking for a total of 20, you should probably invite at least 24.

Better yet, get a pulse from your friends beforehand to make sure they're going to be around. It can be a drag to fully plan a party and send out invitations only to find out everyone's already going to Sue's party down the street!

Next, make sure the people you invite all get along. Many a party has turned into an all-out disaster due to warring factions of friends — and you definitely don't want to have to play referee at your own fiesta!

Last but not least, if it's a boy-girl gathering, try to invite equal numbers of both, so no one feels uncomfortable.

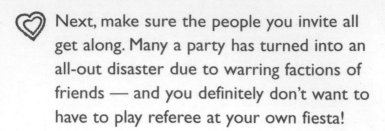

CHOOSING A THEME

Now here's the fun part! Once you've got the general type of event and guest list figured out, it's time to choose a theme.

This is where your true style comes into play — so go nuts! Your theme should carry over in everything from your invitations to your decorations, favors, music choices, and more! There's no limit to the fun you can have with a theme — it just takes a little creativity and some planning.

Are you a retro-movie buff? Plan a movie-themed gathering and feature a few of your fave classics. Try creating invitations that look like movie tickets, serve popcorn, and traditional movie-theater fare, play music from your favorite sound tracks — you can even have friends come dressed up as their favorite movie stars!

☞ Or how about a makeover party with your BFFs? Make invitations out of lipstick (no, don't write with the lipstick, use it to hold the invite!). Write out the invitation details on a scroll of paper and wrap it around the outside of an inexpensive lipstick, tie with a glittery ribbon, and hand deliver! Ask each friend to bring a bottle of nail polish — give each other full-fledged manicures.

☞ Have beauty mags lying around for inspiration. You can make some of the body scrubs, lip balm, or body lotions from chapter 4! You could even have each girl bring a couple of articles of clothing that they don't wear and have a clothes swap.

No matter what your interests are, you can always create a theme that will just scream "you!"

Invitations

The invitations are usually the first point of contact with your guests and where they'll get the first impression of what kind of fun affair awaits. The great thing is invitations don't have to be traditional cards and envelopes — you can make almost anything related to your theme into an invitation!

Having a beach party? Write your invitation on the inside of large seashells!

A dance party? Cut out invitations in the shape of CDs and put in CD cases — (cheap and easy to find at music stores).

Let your theme be your inspiration! Never underestimate the power of the invitation to set the tone for your get-together!

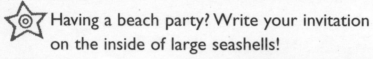

Invitation essentials

Here's the essential info you need to include in any invitation.

❀ Party type (Is it a birthday, Hawaiian luau, sleepover?)
❀ Date

🌸 Time

🌸 Location (Your address, or if you're having it somewhere else, make sure you give the info on the place!)

🌸 RSVP info (so you know how many people are coming well in advance of the big day. This will impact how much food you need, etc!)

Also include any special instructions related to the theme. For example, for a dance party you might ask everyone to bring their fave CD, or ask them to wear their favorite hat for an afternoon tea.

PREPARATION

Prepare, prepare, prepare! Don't wait until the day of your party to do the shopping and decorating — that's a surefire recipe for one totally stressed-out hostess. Instead, make a list of everything you'll need at least a few days in advance and try to do as much prep work as possible in the days leading up to your event. Ask your family for help getting everything together — so you're not still putting together that awesome party CD when your guests arrive!

Sample party timeline for a sleepover party:

Party timeline

6:00	— put out some snacks and start the music
6:15	— guests begin to arrive
6:15–6:45	— continue greeting guests
6:45–7:30	— craft time!
7:30–8:15	— pizza, pizza, pizza!
8:15–10:15	— movie time
10:15–10:45	— ice-cream break
10:45–11:30	— dance party!
11:30–1:00	— movie #2
1:00	— light's out! (yeah, right!)

A timeline will help you keep things running smoothly — but the big thing to remember is not to freak out if things go off schedule! If your friends are having a blast creating coil bracelets, you don't want to stop them mid-bead just because it's "time" for the next activity.

Always try to be aware of the crowd — and be flexible! And more than anything, be

sure not to panic if something goes wrong. The secret of a good hostess is to be able to think on her feet. Pizza delivery late? Don't worry! No one will know the difference if you keep your cool and just keep up the tunes!

Party time!

The day has finally arrived! Relax and enjoy — you've done the prep work, now it's time to have some fun. Good food, good guests, good music, and a cool theme — what more could a preteen girl want?

TIP: Make sure no one feels left out! Someone sitting alone? Be sure to include them in a convo!

Looking for some more fun party themes? Check out these festive ideas for your next soiree — recipes included!

HAWAIIAN LUAU
party

Say "aloha" to a fun summer luau! Traditional Hawaiian luaus were feasts designed to help natives communicate with the gods. Today, they're a great way to bring the fun of the tropics to your backyard. Even if you're miles away from the nearest ocean, you can still enjoy hosting a tropical "island" party!

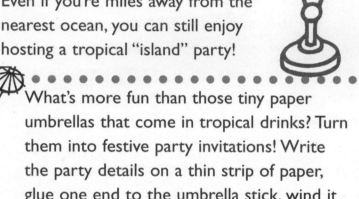

What's more fun than those tiny paper umbrellas that come in tropical drinks? Turn them into festive party invitations! Write the party details on a thin strip of paper, glue one end to the umbrella stick, wind it around, and tie with a ribbon.

Get some groovy surfer tunes (Beach Boys, anyone?) to get everyone in total island mode.

Decorate with tiki torches and pineapples and offer leis and grass skirts from a local

party store for all your friends — even the guys! Or find out how to make your own on page 131!

● ● ● ● ● ● ● ● ● ● ● ● ● ● ● ● ● ● ● ●
Looking for a fun activity? Why not try coconut bowling? Set up some plastic drinks bottles and try for some strikes using a coconut for a bowling ball. The limbo or a conga line are always crowd favorites, too! Or best yet, how about a group hula? Pick up an instruction book from your local library!

● ● ● ● ● ● ● ● ● ● ● ● ● ● ● ● ● ● ● ●
Girls-only gathering? Offer flowered flip-flops or blooming ponytail holders for prizes and/or favors!

● ● ● ● ● ● ● ● ● ● ● ● ● ● ● ● ● ● ● ●
Make an explosive volcano sundae dessert! Mound chocolate ice cream into the shape of a volcano, scoop out the center part and fill with chocolate sauce and strawberry topping, allowing it to drip over the sides. Just make sure to serve immediately, otherwise you'll have a heaping pile of melted lava soup!

DIY *decorations!*

Homemade leis

Leis are flowered "necklaces," traditionally made from fresh flowers and offered as a greeting to guests. Now you can create your own with a bit of construction paper and a few beads!

Materials list (makes 1 lei)
- ✔ Colored paper
- ✔ Miscellaneous medium-sized beads
- ✔ String
- ✔ Scissors
- ✔ Needle
- ✔ One 40-inch piece of embroidery thread

1 Cut out fifty to sixty 2-inch paper flower shapes.

2 Thread the needle and make a knot at the end.

3 Push the needle through one flower, add a bead, then repeat and continue the

pattern until you have 2 inches
of string left.

4 Tie the two ends together with a
knot to close your lei.

5 Place a lei over the head of
each guest as they arrive. Make sure to give the
lei with a traditional Hawaiian kiss on the cheek!

Grass skirt

How can you hula without a grass skirt? Now
you can make your own using raffia from a
craft store for some hip-shaking fun!

Materials list
- ✔ Raffia (the longer the
  strands the better)
- ✔ Scissors

1 Knot together several pieces of raffia to be
used as the belt. (The "belt" should fit below
your waist and rest on the hips.) Leave the
final ends untied for the time being.

2 Tie a piece of raffia onto the belt making sure the knot is in the middle so two equal lengths of "grass" hang down.

3 Repeat with more strands of raffia, tying along the belt.

4 Tie the ends of the belt around your waist and start dancing Hawaiian-style!

Check out these island recipes sure to be total crowd-pleasers (and pleasing to the hostess, too, since they're pretty easy to make!).

Island slush

ADULT HELP NEEDED!

This tropical drink recipe is especially great because you can make most of it beforehand and keep it in the freezer!

Ingredients:

- ✔ 5 cups water
- ✔ 2 tablespoons sugar
- ✔ 6 1/4 cups mango nectar
- ✔ 6 1/4 cups pineapple juice
- ✔ 7 1/4 cups ginger ale

1 Bring 2 cups of the water and sugar to boil in medium saucepan. Boil for approximately 3 minutes.

2 In a large glass or plastic bowl, combine the sugar mixture, pineapple juice, mango nectar, and 3 cups of water. Cover the bowl with plastic wrap and freeze.

3 Thaw slightly before serving. For every glass of slush, add a half glass of ginger ale!

Of course, you might want to garnish with those tiny tropical drink umbrellas, pineapple slices, and cherries!

Makes 14 servings

Tropical kebabs

No luau would be complete without our tropical grilled kebabs! Use bamboo skewers for an authentic touch — just be sure to soak them before cooking!

ADULT HELP NEEDED!

Ingredients:
- ✔ 1 3/4 pounds beef (sirloin tip or shoulder steak works well)
- ✔ 1 cup pineapple juice
- ✔ Juice of 1 lime
- ✔ 1 small onion, finely chopped
- ✔ 2 cloves crushed garlic
- ✔ 1 teaspoon chopped fresh ginger
- ✔ 1/4 teaspoon Tabasco sauce

1 Cut beef into ¾-inch cubes.

2 Mix the remaining ingredients in a bowl large enough to hold the beef.

3 Add the beef and cover with plastic wrap. Refrigerate overnight.

4 Slide the beef on skewers, leaving a small space between each piece.

5 Grill or fry for about 15 minutes, turning often.

Easy noodle salad

Once you get past the prep work (get Mom or Dad to help with the slicing and dicing!), this salad favorite is a cinch! Looking to spice things up? Try adding a dash of crushed red pepper for some extra zing!

ADULT HELP NEEDED!

Ingredients:
- ✔ 3 tablespoons vegetable oil
- ✔ 3 tablespoons rice vinegar
- ✔ 1 1/2 tablespoons soy sauce
- ✔ 1 tablespoon sesame oil
- ✔ 2 garlic cloves
- ✔ 2 teaspoons minced ginger
- ✔ 1 teaspoon sugar
- ✔ 1/2 teaspoon Tabasco sauce
- ✔ 2 small onions, sliced
- ✔ 1 carrot, peeled and grated
- ✔ 1/2 cucumber, peeled, chopped
- ✔ 2 tablespoons chopped fresh coriander
- ✔ 1 pound linguine or angel hair pasta

1 Mix all the ingredients (except pasta) together in a large bowl. Refrigerate at least one hour.

2 Cook the pasta according to the package instructions, and drain. Rinse with cold water.

3 Spoon the mixture over the pasta for a healthy feast to go with your kebabs!

Makes 4 servings
Difficulty rating ✂ ✂

Coconut custard

After one taste of this creamy coconut custard, your guests will be transported to the shores of Waikiki!

ADULT HELP NEEDED!

Ingredients:
✔ 2 cups coconut milk
✔ 1 cup of water
✔ 4 tablespoons sugar
✔ 2 tablespoons cornstarch
✔ 1/2 teaspoon vanilla extract
✔ Pinch of salt

1 In a medium saucepan, combine water, coconut milk, and sugar. Slowly mix in cornstarch, vanilla, and salt.

2 Cook on medium heat, stirring constantly until thickened.

3 Pour into a greased 8 x 8-inch cake pan and chill for at least 1 hour.

4 Cut into squares to serve!

Makes 12 servings

CHOCOLATE DECADENCE
party

Have a chocolate obsession? Who doesn't love that sweet, dark, decadent treat?! Celebrate your love for this luscious goodie with a complete Chocolate Decadence party! Check out these ideas for a cocoa-rific party! (And whatever you do, just make sure you have plenty of ice-cold milk on hand!)

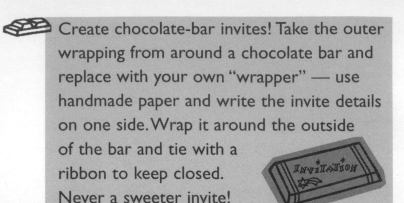 Create chocolate-bar invites! Take the outer wrapping from around a chocolate bar and replace with your own "wrapper" — use handmade paper and write the invite details on one side. Wrap it around the outside of the bar and tie with a ribbon to keep closed. Never a sweeter invite!

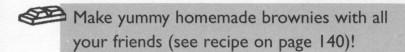 Make yummy homemade brownies with all your friends (see recipe on page 140)!

Serve a chocolate fondue — cut up some bananas, strawberries, and other fruits — and dip!

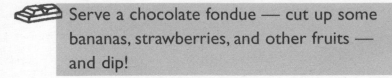 Make chocolate milk and milk shakes or homemade hot cocoa (see recipe below) — depending on the weather.

Rent *Willy Wonka and the Chocolate Factory*, of course!

Give out little bags of chocolate kisses for favors!

Hot chocolate-bar cocoa

Hot chocolate doesn't just come in powdered packets! Here's how you

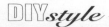

can make the most luscious hot cocoa concoc-
tion ever — using candy bars! Mmmmm, so
rich 'n' creamy you may never go back!

Ingredients:
- ✔ 2-ounce chocolate bar
- ✔ 2 egg yolks (it sounds icky, but tastes great!)
- ✔ 1 cup milk

1 In a small bowl, beat the egg yolks using a
fork.

2 Break up the chocolate into small pieces
and place in a small microwave-safe bowl. Add
the milk.

3 Place the bowl with the chocolate and milk
into the microwave and cook on medium-high
until the chocolate is melted ($2^1/2$ to 3 minutes),
whisking with a fork once or twice while heating.

4 Remove the bowl from the microwave and
slowly pour the chocolate into the beaten egg
yolks, whisking constantly with the fork.

5 Return the mixture into the microwave-safe bowl and cook on medium-high for 1 minute.

6 Pour into mugs and start sipping!

> **TIP:** To separate the egg yolks from the whites, crack the egg in half and gently drop the yolk from one side of the shell to the other, draining the whites into a small bowl or cup as you go!

Makes 4 mugs

Best-ever brownies

These delicious 'n' decadent chocolate brownies are sure to disappear every time you make them!

Ingredients:
- ✔ 1 cup flour
- ✔ 1 cup chopped walnuts
- ✔ 2 cups sugar
- ✔ 1 teaspoon vanilla extract
- ✔ 4 eggs
- ✔ 1/2 teaspoon salt
- ✔ 1/2 cup butter
- ✔ 4 ounces unsweetened chocolate
- ✔ Confectioners' sugar (optional)

1 Preheat oven to 375°F.

2 Butter and lightly dust a 9 x 9 x 3-inch cake pan with flour.

3 Melt the chocolate and butter in a saucepan over low heat. Make sure to stir often!

4 When melted, remove from the heat and cool.

5 Put the eggs, sugar, salt, and vanilla in a mixing bowl and get an adult to beat with an electric mixer for 10 minutes.

6 Stir in the chocolate and butter mixture.

7 Add the flour and stir until all the ingredients are combined, then stir in the walnuts.

8 Using the spatula, spread the mixture into the cake pan and bake for 25 minutes.

9 Once cooked, remove from the oven and allow to cool for at least 1 hour before cutting into squares.

10 Sprinkle with confectioners' sugar and eat up!

> **TIP:** For a super-chocolate indulgence, heap on some chocolate ice cream and hot fudge for a totally chocolaty brownie sundae!

Makes 12 BIG brownies

AFTERNOON TEA
party

You're never too old for a tea party! Get all the girls dressed up for a lovely afternoon tea using the ideas below.

Cut out invitations in the shape of teapots, or turn a dainty paper doily from a party store into a charming invite (you can even include a tea bag inside!).

Dress up the table with delicate teacups and saucers, a floral tablecloth, flowers, and pretty napkins.

Have girls come dressed up in their afternoon finery — and give each a feather boa when they arrive (you know there's lots of stuff they can do with it afterward!).

DIY*style*

Create place cards out of gingerbread-girl cookies (see recipe below). If you're handy with the pastry bag, you can write each girl's name on the cookie with icing or tie a tag around the cookie with each girl's name on one.

Pick up a book on reading tea leaves so you can tell your guests' fortunes when you're done!

All the lovely young ladies invited to your tea are sure to "Oooh" and "Aah" over these pretty and petite afternoon tea treats (not to mention yummy, too!).

Gingerbread girls

Sure, we've all heard of gingerbread men, but our gingerbread girls taste just as yummy — and are even more fun to decorate!

Ingredients:

- ✔ 1/2 cup sugar
- ✔ 1/2 cup black-strap molasses
- ✔ 1 tablespoon milk
- ✔ 3 tablespoons butter
- ✔ 3 1/2 cups flour
- ✔ 1/2 teaspoon each of baking powder, salt, ground nutmeg, ground cinnamon, ground cloves, ground ginger

1 Preheat oven to 350°F. Coat two baking sheets with butter.

2 Heat the molasses in a saucepan until it boils. Remove it from the heat and add the butter, sugar, and milk.

3 In a separate bowl, mix the flour with the salt, cinnamon, nutmeg, ginger, cloves, and baking powder.

4 Add the dry mixture to the molasses and combine well with a fork. If necessary, add a couple of spoonfuls of water, so that the dough sticks together.

5 Sprinkle a dusting of flour on a countertop or cutting board. Roll or pat out the dough so that it's about ¼-inch thick.

6 Ask an adult to cut out large gingerbread girls using a sharp knife and bake for 5 to 7 minutes. (Draw a template on a piece of card stock to trace the knife around.)

7 Remove with oven gloves and allow to cool. Decorate with candy, or ice with our scrumptious icing recipe below!

Makes 10 large cookies

Foolproof frosting

Ingredients:
- ✔ 1½ cups confectioners' sugar
- ✔ 3 tablespoons hot water
- ✔ Food coloring

1 Add hot water to a bowl and beat in the confectioners' sugar with a fork and continue beating for several minutes until the icing is creamy.

2 To add some color, dip the toothpick into the food coloring and mix into the icing.

3 Spoon into a pastry bag until it's half full and gently squeeze to decorate your gingerbread girls, or make your own pastry bag by twisting and taping waxed paper into a cone shape with a small opening at the end.

 TIP: If you're using a pastry bag, try practicing your decorating skills on waxed paper first!

Lollipop bouquet

This blooming bouquet of colorful lollipops promises to make a charming centerpiece for your next afternoon social!

✔ 5 to 6 lollipops (the globe-shaped ones work best!)
✔ Cellophane paper (clear or colored)
✔ Small rubber bands
✔ Thin, green card stock
✔ Small terra-cotta pot
✔ Styrofoam block
✔ Fabric glue
✔ White glue
✔ Knife, scissors, pencil

1 Cut the cellophane into small squares large enough to fit around the top of your lollipop.

2 Remove the existing wrapper from the lollipop and wrap the cellophane around the top. Secure with a rubber band at the base of the lollipop.

3 Cut out a 3-inch flower template and trace the pattern onto the card, drawing as many patterns as you have lollipops. (Use different-colored card stock for a more colorful bouquet!)

4 Cut out the flower patterns and poke a hole in the center of each with a pencil.

5 Slip the lollipop stick through the hole and push the flower all the way up the stick, so that the lollipop top makes the center of the flower. Secure with a little fabric glue if necessary.

6 Grab an adult to cut a piece of Styrofoam with the knife to fit inside the terra-cotta pot.

7 Cut the green card stock into thin strips and crinkle to create "grass."

8 Apply a layer of glue to the top of the Styrofoam and stick on the crinkled "grass." Allow to dry.

9 Stick the lollipops into the Styrofoam to finish your beautiful (and yummy!) bouquet.

TIP: You can also decorate the outside of the terra-cotta pot with acrylic paints for a more personalized touch!

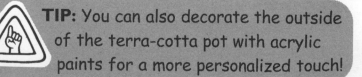

Little finger sandwiches are the staple of any afternoon tea and make for a beautiful presentation when served on a tiered serving tray. Or you can make your own multilevel serving piece by standing one cake-stand on top of another (works best if the top one is a little smaller). And these dainty little sandwiches are even more delectable when cut into fun shapes using ordinary cookie cutters! Use your sandwich favorites like chicken salad, BLTs, or even PB & J — or for something extra-fancy, try the smoked salmon tea sandwich recipe below!

Smoked salmon tea sandwiches

These yummy tea sandwiches are even more fun to eat when cut out in cookie cutter shapes!

Ingredients:
- ✔ 12 thin slices of white sandwich bread, crusts removed
- ✔ 2 ounces dill butter (see recipe on page 150)
- ✔ 6 1/2 ounces thinly sliced smoked salmon

1 Spread the dill butter on one side of each of the bread slices.

2 Layer slices of the smoked salmon evenly across half of the bread slices. Top with the rest of the bread slices.

3 Use a cookie cutter and cut out the tea sandwiches, discarding (or better yet, eating!) the remnants.

Arrange on a serving piece . . . and serve!

Makes 12 sandwiches

Dill butter

Ingredients:
- ✔ 1 ounce cream cheese
- ✔ 4 tablespoons unsalted butter (at room temp.)
- ✔ 1/2 teaspoon lemon zest (see note on next page)
- ✔ 1/2 tablespoon lemon juice
- ✔ 1 tablespoon chopped parsley
- ✔ 1 tablespoon chopped fresh dill
- ✔ Pinch of salt

1 Place all the ingredients in a bowl and mash together with a wooden spoon until completely blended.

2 Roll into a ball and wrap in waxed paper and refrigerate until you're ready to use.

Note: The "zest" of a lemon comes from the peel — if you don't have a lemon zester (not exactly up there with a wooden spoon in terms of common kitchen utensils!), you can grate the peel with a grater. The part that grates off is the zest!

FAR-OUT, FAR EAST
festivity

Looking for something a little more exotic for your next party? Try this fully fashionable, far-out, Far East festivity and bring some of the Orient into your home!

Create invitations out of Japanese paper, which is available at stationery stores. You can even decorate with Japanese characters and include a haiku related to the party! Roll them into scrolls and tie with a ribbon.

Order in takeout or make some of our great Far East–inspired creations below!

 Serve fortune cookies for dessert, or our own fortune-filled meringue kisses (see recipe on page 157).

 Rent some Bruce Lee karate classics or Jackie Chan's latest!

 Make the origami gift box from chapter 5 and fill with sweets for a party favor.

DIY *decorations!*

Paper lanterns

It's easy to make your own paper party lanterns for decorations!

Materials list:
- ✔ Thick red-and-gold paper, rectangular in shape
- ✔ Scissors
- ✔ Hole punch
- ✔ Ribbon

1 Begin by folding each sheet of paper in half lengthwise.

2 Beginning about 1 inch from the top, cut a slit from the fold to within a $1/2$ inch of the end.

3 Repeat at approximately 1-inch intervals, until you are about 1 inch from the bottom of the paper. (You can try it on a scrap of paper — you'll be amazed at how easy it is!)

4 Unfold the sheet of paper and tape the short edges together so you have a cylindrical lantern. Punch two holes at the top to string ribbon through and hang!

Try some of these recipes inspired by the East. And be sure to provide chopsticks for all your guests!

Crab rangoon

Make this take-out favorite in your own kitchen! Better yet, you can prepare them a day ahead of time and pop them in the oven right before your party!

Ingredients:

- ✔ 16 ounces cream cheese
- ✔ 6 1/2 ounces of lumped crab meat, drained
- ✔ 4 spring onions, thinly sliced
- ✔ 2 garlic cloves, crushed
- ✔ 1 tablespoon Worcestershire sauce
- ✔ 1 teaspoon soy sauce
- ✔ 1 pack of wonton skins — (you will need 48 skins, available at Asian markets or in the Asian food section of most supermarkets)
- ✔ Vegetable cooking spray

1 Heat the oven to 425°F. In a medium-sized bowl, combine everything except the wonton skins (and vegetable spray!). Mix until well blended.

2 Place a spoonful of filling in the center of each wonton skin. Moisten two connecting edges of the wonton skin, pull the other two edges over to form a triangle, and seal. Fold the two opposite corners up slightly.

3 Lightly coat a baking sheet with vegetable spray. Arrange your rangoon on the sheet and lightly coat with vegetable spray.

4 Bake in the oven for 12 to 15 minutes or until golden-brown. Serve alone or with sweet-and-sour sauce.

Makes 48 crab rangoon

TIP: Make sure the cream cheese is softened before you try to mix it!

Edamame

Otherwise known as the ultra-healthy soybean, edamame is a yummy (and healthy) alternative to chips — and so easy to prepare. You can find edamame in the frozen section of any health food store.

ADULT HELP NEEDED!

Ingredients:
- ✔ Water
- ✔ Edamame
- ✔ Salt

I Bring the water to a boil in a medium saucepan.

2 Add edamame and cook according to the package directions (approximately four minutes).

3 Drain, sprinkle on some salt, and serve!

Yummy chicken dumplings

ADULT HELP NEEDED!

Ingredients:
- ✔ 1 pound ground chicken breast
- ✔ 2 chopped scallions
- ✔ 2 tablespoons soy sauce
- ✔ Salt and pepper to taste
- ✔ 1 tablespoon sesame oil
- ✔ 1/2 cup chicken broth
- ✔ Eight 3 × 6-inch square egg-roll wrappers

1 Combine the chicken, soy sauce, salt, pepper, and green onions in a large bowl.

2 Mix well and divide into 8 equal portions.

3 Place each portion in the center of an egg-roll wrapper.

4 Moisten the edges with water and pull up

all four corners to meet in the center. Pinch together to seal.

5 Heat the oil in large nonstick pan over medium heat.

6 Get an adult to fry the dumplings, flat side down, for 2 minutes, or until golden-brown on the bottom.

7 Add the broth, cover, and steam for 5 minutes.

8 Serve soy sauce on the side — yum!

Makes 8 dumplings

Meringue kisses

In place of fortune cookies, try these meringue kisses with a message all of their own! Just make sure you give yourself plenty of time (you'll see why!).

ADULT HELP NEEDED!

Ingredients:
✔ 1 teaspoon vanilla extract
✔ 5 tablespoons sugar
✔ 2 egg whites

1 Preheat the oven to 250°F, then cover a baking sheet with waxed paper.

2 Beat the egg whites with an electric beater in a bowl until stiff (they should "peak" when you pull the beaters away).

3 Add 3 tablespoons of the sugar, one spoonful at a time, beating well after each spoonful.

4 Add the vanilla and then spoon in the remaining 2 tablespoons of sugar.

5 Drop the meringues onto the baking sheet using a spoon and shape so they form "kisses."

6 Bake for 1 hour, then turn off the oven and let the meringues remain inside the oven for 6 (yes, 6!) hours until they are dry and crisp. (You might be tempted to peek inside — but don't, it will hurt the consistency!)

7 Once dry, wrap the individual kisses in squares of colored tissue paper

and tuck in a slip of paper with a fortune for an extra-fun party favor!

 TIP: Make sure the eggs are at room temperature before you beat them.

Makes 12 meringues

I gave these to all my friends at my last sleepover party. They all wanted to know how I made them!

Helyne, 10

IT'S A WRAP!

So now you've got the know-how to cut, glue, sew, or bake your way to your own particular brand of DIY Style! But don't stop here! With a dash of creativity, a heaping helping of confidence, and a healthy dose of patience, there's no limit to the stylish goodies a true style guru like you can create. There's a universe of ideas waiting to be discovered all around you! Try looking for inspiration in everyday objects — pretty papers, fun fabrics, ribbons, paints, beads — even a trip to the hardware store can end up turning the most ordinary objects into total treasures! And if your projects don't always come out looking like they belong on Rodeo Drive — don't worry! The key is that no matter what you do, your style will come through. So next time you're flip-ping through one of your fave mags and see something you absolutely, positively cannot make it through the next week of school without — make it better (and cheaper!) — *just do it yourself!*